THE LAWYER'S QUOTATION BOOK

A County Court.

By the same author

Why Not Live in Spain?
Discovering Spanish Wine
Living in Spain Today
Living in Spain in the Eighties
Living in Spain
Spanish Real Property and Inheritance Laws

The Lawyer's Quotation Book

A Legal Companion

Edited by
JOHN REAY-SMITH

ROBERT HALE · LONDON

First published in Great Britain 1991

ISBN 0 7090 4474 7

Robert Hale Limited
Clerkenwell House
Clerkenwell Green
London EC1R 0HT

To
MARCELLE

Photoset in Goudy by
Derek Doyle & Associates, Mold, Clwyd.
Printed and bound in Hong Kong

Preface

Law is a serious matter and affects the lives of all of us in one way or another, but it needs to be leavened with laughter. Indeed many jokes about the law and lawyers have been invented by lawyers, just as the best Scottish jokes originate north of the Border.

I have much enjoyed collecting these quotations, and have rediscovered old friends and made many new ones.

In this century F. E. Smith has been one of the most quotable lawyers, and a master of the gladiatorial contest with difficult Judges. Later, as Lord Birkenhead, he became a reforming Lord Chancellor, and revolutionized the laws of real property. Charles Dickens, Anthony Trollope and George Bernard Shaw have also provided memorable legal quotations.

However, my greatest thanks are due to William Shakespeare, who has been the source of more material than any other writer. What a profound understanding he had of the law and lawyers – 'their quiddities and tricks'.

I have included some three hundred entries which span four thousand years, and hope that readers will discover many that they like, both wise and amusing, and perhaps will find opportunities to use them.

John Reay-Smith

THE OLD HALL OF THE INNER TEMPLE

The first thing we do, let's kill all the lawyers.
WILLIAM SHAKESPEARE
Henry VI, Part 2

The law and medicine should be very serious professions to undertake, should they not? People's lives and fortunes depend on them.
GEORGE ELIOT

The law is the true embodiment
Of everything that's excellent.
It has no kind of fault or flaw
And I, my Lords, embody the law.
W.S. GILBERT
Iolanthe

Inner for the rich; Middle for the poor;
Lincoln's Inn for chancery, and Gray's Inn for the boor.
ANONYMOUS

It is night in Lincoln's Inn – perplexed and troublous valley of the shadow of the Law, where suitors generally find but little day.
CHARLES DICKENS
Bleak House

A saying in the Inner Temple: – Life at the bar is not a bed of roses. It is all roses and no bed, or all bed and no roses.

quoted by PHILIP SEPTIMUS PITT

Lawsuit, n. a machine which you go into as a pig and come out as a sausage.

AMBROSE BIERCE
The Devil's Dictionary

It ain't no sin to crack a few laws now and then, just so long as you don't break any.

MAE WEST

There's no better way of exercising the imagination than the study of law. No poet ever interpreted nature as freely as a lawyer interprets truth.

JEAN GIRAUDOUX

A liar should have a good memory.

QUINTILIAN

We wouldn't have been nicked if you'd kept your mouth shut. Making us look ridiculous by telling the truth. Why can't you lie like a normal man?

JOE ORTON
Loot

I do not mind lying, but I hate inaccuracy.

SAMUEL BUTLER

Law is a bottomless pit.

DR JOHN ARBUTHNOT

Lincoln's Inn.

Mr. Pickwick and Sam in the Attorney's Office

No amount of eloquence will make an English lawyer think that loyalty to truth should come before loyalty to his client.

ANTHONY TROLLOPE
Orley Farm

No brilliance is needed in the law. Nothing but common sense, and relatively clean fingernails.

JOHN MORTIMER

One with the law is a majority.

CALVIN COOLIDGE

Good men must not obey the laws too much.

RALPH WALDO EMERSON

If the law supposes that, said Mr Bumble, the law is a ass – a idiot.

CHARLES DICKENS

The Common Law of England has very laboriously been built about a mythical figure of 'the reasonable man'. An Act of God has been defined as 'something which no reasonable man could have expected'.

A.P. HERBERT

When we hear that the son of a washerwoman has become Lord Chancellor or Archbishop of Canterbury, we do, theoretically and abstractedly, feel a higher reverence for such a self-made magnate than for one who has been, as it were, born into forensic or ecclesiastical purple.

ANTHONY TROLLOPE
Orley Farm

Judge: 'Poor boy – poor boy – blind. Put him on a chair so that the jury can see him.'

F.E.: 'Perhaps your Honour would like to have the boy passed round the jury box.'

Judge: 'That is a most improper remark.'

F.E.: 'It was provoked by a most improper suggestion.'

Judge: 'Mr Smith, have you ever heard of a saying by Bacon – the great Bacon – that youth and discretion are ill-wedded companions.'

F.E.: 'Yes, I have. And have you ever heard of a saying by Bacon – the great Bacon – that a much talking Judge is like an ill-tuned cymbal?'

Judge: 'You are extremely offensive, young man.'

F.E.: 'As a matter of fact we both are, and the only difference between us is that I am trying to be, and you can't help it.'

F.E. SMITH

In a case where the young F.E. Smith was briefed by a tram company, a boy alleged that, as a result of being run over by a tram, he had become blind.

That one hundred and fifty lawyers should do business together ought not to be expected.

THOMAS JEFFERSON

I know we're living in a country where respect for the law is proverbial: who'd give power of arrest to the traffic lights if three women magistrates and a Liberal MP would only suggest it.

JOE ORTON
Loot

He is always breaking the law. He broke the law when he was born: his parents were not married.

GEORGE BERNARD SHAW
Major Barbara

They have no lawyers among them, for they consider them as a sort of people whose profession is to disguise matters.

SIR THOMAS MORE

A shell for thee – And a shell for thee – But the oyster is the lawyer's fee.

THOMAS LEWIS INGRAM

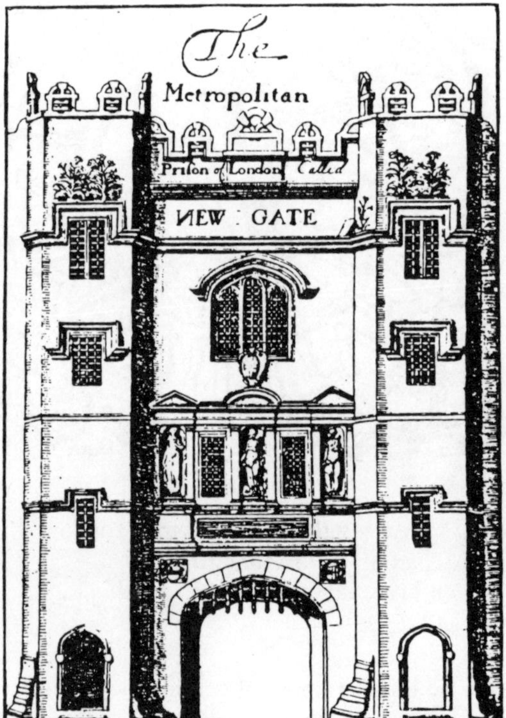

NEWGATE AT THE TIME OF THE PROTECTORATE.

When there is a rift in the lute, the business of the lawyer is to widen the rift and gather the loot.

ARTHUR GARFIELD HAYS

The lawyers have twisted it into such a state of bedevilment that the original merits of the case have long disappeared from the face of the earth. It's about a Will, and the trusts under a Will – or it was once. It's about nothing but Costs now.

CHARLES DICKENS
Bleak House

A solicitor's account.
To my professional charges for crossing the street to greet you, and on discovering that it was not you, crossing the street again. 25 guineas.

ANONYMOUS

Apart from cheese and tulips, the main product of the country is advocaat, a drink made from lawyers.

ALAN COREN
on Holland

They argued from history. They said that no criminal laws had ever been known to prevail against cheek and plausibility such as yours, combined with the power of the long purse.

KENNETH GRAHAME
The Wind in the Willows, Rat tells Toad that Mole and Badger expected him to escape from prison.

In my youth, said his father, I took to the law,
And argued each case with my wife:
And the muscular strength, which it gave to my jaw,
Has lasted the rest of my life.

LEWIS CARROLL

You want justice, but do you want to pay for it? When you go to a butcher you know you have to pay, but you people go to a judge as if you were off to a funeral supper.

BERTOLT BRECHT

The lawyer who acts for himself has a fool for a client.

ANONYMOUS

When the President does it, that means that it is not illegal.

RICHARD NIXON

It is illegal to make liquor privately or water publicly.

LORD BIRKETT

When you have told anyone that you have left him a legacy, the only decent thing is to die at once.

SAMUEL BUTLER

Lawyers' houses are built on the heads of fools.

ANONYMOUS

So when any of the four pillars of government are mainly shaken or weakened (which are religion, justice, counsel and treasure), men have need to pray for fair weather.

SIR FRANCIS BACON

HALE.

From an original Picture in the Library
of Lincoln's Inn

Under the Superintendance of the Society for the Diffusion of Useful Knowledge

London, Published by Charles Knight Ludgate Street & Pall Mall East

Yr most Affle Father
Northington
Grainge
18 Feb 1770
London Published by John Murray, Albemarle Street 1831

I will not say with Lord Hale, that 'The Law will admit of no rival' ... but I will say that it is a jealous mistress, and requires a long and constant courtship. It is not to be won by trifling favours, but by lavish homage.

JOSEPH STORY

Reason is the life of the law: nay, the common law itself is nothing else but reason ... The law which is the perfection of reason.

SIR EDWARD COKE

Take a note of that; his Lordship says he will turn it over in what he is pleased to call his mind.

RICHARD BETHELL

If I were asked what point I'd best like to have in my favour I'd say, a deaf judge. Or if not that, one regularly tired out.

ANTHONY TROLLOPE
Orley Farm

The life of the law has not been logic; it has been reason.

OLIVER WENDELL HOLMES

Lloyd George was not considered good enough with his hands to follow his uncle as a cobbler, so his family decided to make him a lawyer.

ANONYMOUS

Law-makers should not be law-breakers.

ANONYMOUS

Wherever Law ends, Tyranny begins.

JOHN LOCKE

The common law is not a brooding omnipresence in the sky but the articulate voice of some sovereign or quasi-sovereign that can be identified.

OLIVER WENDELL HOLMES

Our defence is not in armaments, nor in science, nor in going underground. Our defence is in law and order.

ALBERT EINSTEIN

Litigious terms, fat contentions, and flowing fees.

JOHN MILTON

The more laws, the more offenders.

ANONYMOUS

A sergeant of the Laws ...
Discreet he was, and of great reverence ...
Nowher so bisy a man as he ther nas:
And yet he seemed bisier than he was.

GEOFFREY CHAUCER

And do as adversaries do in law,
Strive mightily, but eat and drink as friends.

WILLIAM SHAKESPEARE
The Taming of the Shrew

'Let the jury consider their verdict,' the King said, for about the twentieth time that day.

'No, no!' said the Queen. 'Sentence first – verdict afterwards.'

LEWIS CARROLL

OLD SERJEANTS' INN

Interior of Temple Church

The quality of mercy is not strained,
It droppeth as the gentle rain from heaven
Upon the place beneath: it is twice blessed;
It blesses him that gives and him that takes.

WILLIAM SHAKESPEARE
The Merchant of Venice

Fresh from brawling Courts
And dusty purlieus of the law.

ALFRED, LORD TENNYSON

The law embodies the story of a nation's development through many centuries, and it cannot be dealt with as if it contained only the axioms and corollaries of a book of mathematics.

OLIVER WENDELL HOLMES

It is far better that ten guilty persons escape than one innocent suffer.

SIR WILLIAM BLACKSTONE

In respect of civil rights, all citizens are equal before the law. The humblest is the peer of the most powerful.

JOHN MARSHALL HARLAN

All classes are criminal today. We live in an age of equality.

JOE ORTON
Loot

Justice is the only worship.

ROBERT GREEN INGERSOLL

The first law for the historian is that he shall never dare utter an untruth. The second is that he shall suppress nothing that is true.

CICERO

A lawyer without history or literature is a mechanic, a mere working mason: If he possesses some knowledge of these, he may venture to call himself an architect.

SIR WALTER SCOTT

It is not what a lawyer tells me I may do; but what humanity, reason, and justice, tell me I ought to do.

EDMUND BURKE

Deceive not thy physician, confessor, nor lawyer.

GEORGE HERBERT

A bronzed lank man! His suit of ancient black,
A famous high hat and plain worn shawl,
Make him the quaint great figure that men love,
The prairie-lawyer, master of us all.

N. VACHEL LINDSAY

Now these are the Laws of the Jungle, and many and mighty are they;
But the head and the hoof of the Law, and the haunch and the hump, is – Obey!

RUDYARD KIPLING

The law: It has honoured us; may we honour it.

DANIEL WEBSTER

1658
30 Inches High. 25 do Wide.
JANE, LADY CÆSAR;
Daughter of Sir Edward Barkham, Knt.
Lord Mayor of London in 1622;
And Wife of Sir Charles Cæsar, Knt. Master of the Rolls;
Married 1626; Died June 16th 1661, aged 66;
Buried at Bennington in Herts.
Robt. Wilkinson

Master's House
from Inner Temple.

Great cases like hard cases make bad law.

OLIVER WENDELL HOLMES

The law hath not been dead, though it hath slept.

WILLIAM SHAKESPEARE
Measure for Measure

Draw up the papers, lawyer, and make 'em good and stout,
For things at home are crossways, and Betsy and I are out,
... And so we've agreed together that we can't never agree.

WILLIAM CARLETON

Ignorance of the law excuses no man; not that all men know the law, but because 'tis an excuse every man will plead, and no man can tell how to refute him.

JOHN SELDON

The meanest citizen, actuated by the meanest motives, is entitled to insist upon the enforcement of the law. The question is, 'What is the law?' a question which frequently arises in our Courts and sometimes receives a satisfactory answer.

A.P. HERBERT

Why may not that be the skull of a lawyer? Where may be his quiddities now, his quillets, his cases, his tenures, and his tricks?

WILLIAM SHAKESPEARE
Hamlet

Who happens to be in the Lord Chancellor's Court this murky afternoon besides the Lord Chancellor, the counsel in the cause, two or three counsel who are never in any cause, and the well of solicitors before mentioned?

CHARLES DICKENS
Bleak House

And, through the heat of conflict, keeps the law
In calmness made, and sees what he foresaw.

WILLIAM WORDSWORTH

The aim of forensic oratory is to teach, to delight, to move.

CICERO

A nation may be said to consist of its territory, its people, and its laws. The territory is the only part which is of certain durability.

ABRAHAM LINCOLN

All religions, laws, moral and political systems are but necessary means to preserve social order.

CH'EN TU-HSIU

How small, of all that human hearts endure,
That part which laws or kings can cause or cure!

SAMUEL JOHNSON

Even when laws have been written down, they ought not always to remain unaltered.

ARISTOTLE

Government implies the power of making laws. It is essential to the idea of a law, that it be attended with a sanction; or, in other words, a penalty or punishment for disobedience.

ALEXANDER HAMILTON

The chess board is the world, the pieces are the phenomena of the universe, the rules of the game are what we call the laws of Nature. The player on the other side is hidden from us. We know that his play is always fair, just and patient. But also we know, to our cost, that he never overlooks a mistake, or makes the smallest allowance for ignorance.

THOMAS HENRY HUXLEY

COGERS' HALL, FROM AN OLD PRINT

The law, in its majestic equality, forbids the rich as well as the poor to sleep under bridges, to beg in the streets, and to steal bread.

ANATOLE FRANCE

Law is order, and good law is good order.

ARISTOTLE

The law is the last result of human wisdom acting upon human experience for the benefit of the public.

SAMUEL JOHNSON

We learn how to behave as lawyers, soldiers, merchants, or whatnot by being them. Life, not the parson, teaches conduct.

OLIVER WENDELL HOLMES

Let us remember that if we suffer tamely a lawless attack upon our liberty, we encourage it, and involve others in our doom.

SAMUEL ADAMS

Equity is a roguish thing. For Law we have a measure, know what to trust to; Equity is according to the conscience of him that is Chancellor, and as that is larger or narrower, so is Equity. 'Tis all one as if they should make the standard for the measure we call a 'foot' a Chancellor's foot; what an uncertain measure! One Chancellor has a long foot, another a short foot, a third an indifferent foot. 'Tis the same thing in the Chancellor's conscience.

JOHN SELDON

Equity sends questions to Law. Law sends questions back to Equity; Law finds it can't do this, Equity finds it can't do that; neither can so much as say it can't do anything, without this solicitor instructing and this counsel appearing for A, and that solicitor instructing and that counsel appearing for B.

CHARLES DICKENS
Bleak House

In law, what plea so tainted and corrupt
But, being seasoned with a gracious voice,
Obscures the show of evil?

WILLIAM SHAKESPEARE
The Merchant of Venice

Lesser breeds without the Law.

RUDYARD KIPLING

The law locks up both man and woman
Who steals the goose from the common,
But lets the greater felon loose
Who steals the common from the goose.

EDWARD POTTS CHEYNEY

There is no grievance that is a fit object of redress by mob law.

ABRAHAM LINCOLN

Necessity hath no law. Feigned necessities, imagined necessities ... are the greatest cozenage that men can put upon the Providence of God, and make pretences to break known rules by.

OLIVER CROMWELL

Necessity knows no law except to prevail.

PUBLILIUS SYRUS

Law will never be strong or respected unless it has the sentiment of the people behind it. If the people of a state make bad laws, they will suffer for it. They will be the first to suffer. Suffering, and nothing else, will implant that sentiment of responsibility which is the first step to reform.

JAMES BRYCE

No written law has ever been more binding than unwritten custom supported by popular opinion.

CARRIE CHAPMAN CATT

Old Doorway
LAMB COURT

Sr Beniamin Rudyerd Surveyor of his Maties Court of Wardes and Li= ueries

Pub Nov 1 1796 by W Richardson No 31 Strand.

No man is above the law and no man is below it; nor do we ask any man's permission when we require him to obey it. Obedience to the law is demanded as a right; not asked as a favour.

THEODORE ROOSEVELT

The law ... will not bend to the uncertain wishes, imaginations and wanton tempers of men ... On the one hand it is inexorable to the cries and lamentations of the prisoners; on the other it is deaf, deaf as an adder, to the clamours of the populace.

JOHN ADAMS

De minitas non curat lox – The law is not concerned with trifles.

LEGAL MAXIM

We must not make a scarecrow of the law,
Setting it up to fear the birds of prey,
And let it keep one shape, till custom make it
Their perch, and not their terror.

WILLIAM SHAKESPEARE
Measure for Measure

Only our concept of time makes it possible for us to speak of the Day of Judgement by that name; in reality it is a summary court in perpetual session.

FRANZ KAFKA

There is but one law for all, namely, that law which governs all law, the law of our Creator, the law of humanity, justice, equity – the law of nature, and of nations.

EDMUND BURKE

No freeman shall be taken, or imprisoned, or outlawed, or exiled, or in any way harmed, nor will we go upon him nor will we send upon him, except by the legal judgement of his peers or by the law of the land.

MAGNA CARTA

Nor shall any person be subject for the same offence to be twice put in jeopardy of life or limb; nor shall be compelled in any criminal case to be a witness against himself; nor be deprived of life, liberty, or property without due process of law.

THE CONSTITUTION OF THE UNITED STATES OF AMERICA, fifth amendment

Law: an ordinance of reason for the common good, made by him who has care of the community.

ST THOMAS AQUINAS

The people should fight for their law as for a wall.

HERACLITUS

The people's good is the highest law.

CICERO

Possession is eleven points in the law.

COLLEY CIBBER

One precedent creates another. They soon accumulate and constitute law. What yesterday was fact, today is doctrine.

JUNIUS
Letters

Inner Temple
Library

THE HALL OF GRAY'S INN.

Public opinion's always in advance of the law.
JOHN GALSWORTHY

Laws grind the poor, and rich men rule the law.
OLIVER GOLDSMITH

Six hours in sleep, in law's grave study six,
Four spend in prayer, the rest on nature fix.
SIR EDWARD COKE

He has his law degree and a furnished office. It's just a question now of getting him out of bed.
PETER ARNO

The law must be stable, but it must not stand still.
ROSCOE POUND

This law which is the spirit of law is the opposite of an accumulation of old precedents and new fiats. By this higher law, that men must not be arbitrary, the old law is continually tested and the new law reviewed.
WALTER LIPPMAN

The prophecies of what the courts will do in practice, and nothing more pretentious, are what I mean by the law.
OLIVER WENDELL HOLMES

Who to himself is law no law doth need,
Offends no law, and is a king indeed.
GEORGE CHAPMAN

We have talked long enough in this country about equal rights. We have talked for a hundred years or more. It is time now to write in the next chapter – and to write in the books of law.

LYNDON JOHNSON

Laws and police regulations can be compared to a spider's web that lets the big mosquitoes through and catches the small ones.

JULIUS WILHELM ZINCGREF

The one great principle of the English law is, to make business for itself. There is no other principle distinctly, certainly, and consistently maintained through all its narrow turnings.

CHARLES DICKENS
Bleak House

T' abhor the makers, and their laws approve,
Is to hate traitors and the treason love.

JOHN DRYDEN

When you break the big laws, you do not get liberty; you do not even get anarchy. You get the small laws.

G.K. CHESTERTON

Laws are sand, customs are rock. Laws can be evaded and punishment escaped, but an openly transgressed custom brings sure punishment.

MARK TWAIN

Good laws lead to the making of better ones, bad ones bring about worse.

JEAN JACQUES ROUSSEAU

Cut-Brick Portal
in King's Bench Walk.

The best use of laws is to teach men to trample bad laws under their feet.

WENDELL PHILLIPS

Unlimited power is apt to corrupt the minds of those who possess it; and this I know, my Lords, that where laws end, tyranny begins.

WILLIAM PITT, EARL OF CHATHAM

... Twelve honest men have decided the cause,
And were judges of facts, though not judges of laws.

SIR WILLIAM PULTENEY

'I'll be judge, I'll be jury,' said cunning old Fury;
'I'll try the whole cause, and condemn you to death.'

LEWIS CARROLL

My object all sublime
I shall achieve in time –
To make the punishment fit the crime.

W.S. GILBERT
The Mikado

The jury, passing on the prisoner's life,
May, in the sworn twelve have a thief or two
Guiltier than him they try.

WILLIAM SHAKESPEARE
Measure for Measure

Whoever desires to found a state and give it laws, must start with assuming that all men are bad and ever ready to display their vicious nature, whenever they may find occasion for it.

NICCOLÒ MACHIAVELLI

I dislike being in the country in August, because my legs get so bitten by barristers.

LYDIA LOPOKOVA

When I was a lad I served a term
As office boy to an Attorney's firm.
I cleaned the windows and I swept the floor
And I polished up the handle of the big front door.
I polished up that handle so carefullee
That now I am the Ruler of the Queen's Navee!

W.S. GILBERT
HMS *Pinafore*

Always remember that when you go into an attorney's office, you will have to pay for it, first or last.

ANTHONY TROLLOPE
Orley Farm

The law is a sort of hocus-pocus science.

CHARLES MACKLIN

Hocus was an old cunning attorney.

DR JOHN ARBUTHNOT

Any government is free to the people under it where the laws rule and the people are a party to the laws.

WILLIAM PENN

For my part I think it a less evil that some criminals should escape than that the government should play an ignoble part.

OLIVER WENDELL HOLMES

A Bit from
Essex Court.

A bumper of good liquor
Will end a contest quicker
Than justice, judge, or vicar.
RICHARD BRINSLEY SHERIDAN

In case of dissension, never dare to judge till you have heard the other side.
EURIPIDES

When men drink, then they are rich and successful and win lawsuits and are happy and help their friends.

Quickly, bring me a beaker of wine, so that I may wet my mind and say something clever.
ARISTOPHANES

Do what thy manhood bids thee do, from none but self expect applause;
He noblest lives and noblest dies who makes and keeps his self-made laws.
SIR RICHARD FRANCIS BURTON

The more laws and order are made prominent
The more thieves and robbers there will be.
LAO-TZU

A professor said, 'People are not interested in freedom but in ham and eggs.' To which I retorted, 'Ten years in prison with only ham and eggs for breakfast would cure that.'
VIEWPOINT, BBC TV

Anyone who has been to an English public school will always feel comparatively at home in prison. It is the people brought up in the gay intimacy of the slums, who find prison so soul-destroying.
EVELYN WAUGH

I do not know whether laws be right,
or whether laws be wrong.
All that we know who lie in gaol,
is that the wall is strong.
And that each day is like a year.
A year whose days are long.

OSCAR WILDE

Once we are destined to live out our lives in the prison of our mind, our one duty is to furnish it well.

PETER USTINOV

The vilest deeds like poison weeds
Bloom well in prison air:
It is only what is good in man
That wastes and withers there.

OSCAR WILDE

Oh they're taking him to prison for the colour of his hair.

ALFRED EDWARD HOUSMAN

The supreme value is not the future but the present. Whoever builds a house for future happiness builds a prison for the present.

OCTAVIO PAZ

Under a government which imprisons any unjustly, the true place for a just man is also a prison ... the only house in a slave state in which a free man abides with honour.

HENRY DAVID THOREAU

THE TRIAL

BY

CHARLOTTE M. YONGE

ILLUSTRATED BY J. PRIESTMAN ATKINSON

Portion of Screen in Middle Temple Hall

Man is a prisoner who has no right to open the door of his prison and run away ... A man should wait, and not take his own life until God summons him.

PLATO

Self is the only prison that can ever bind a soul.

HENRY VAN DYKE

Stone walls do not a prison make,
Nor iron bars a cage.

RICHARD LOVELACE

Stone walls a prisoner make, but not a slave.

WILLIAM WORDSWORTH

Let us reform our schools, and we shall find little reform needed in our prisons.

JOHN RUSKIN

It [prison] feels like being in hospital without the fear of pain or in the army without fear of war.

LORD KAGAN

Persons attempting to find a motive in this narrative will be prosecuted; persons attempting to find a moral in it will be banished; persons attempting to find a plot in it will be shot. By Order of the Author.

MARK TWAIN
The Adventures of Huckleberry Finn

The Chief Justice was rich, quiet and infamous.

LORD MACAULAY
about Warren Hastings

I wish that I was as cocksure of anything as Tom Macaulay is of everything.

WILLIAM LAMB

Judge: 'I have listened very carefully, Mr Smith, to what you have said, but I am none the wiser.'

F.E.: 'None the wiser perhaps, my Lord, but far better informed.'

F.E. SMITH

What is truth? said jesting Pilate. And would not stay for an answer.

SIR FRANCIS BACON

Nor is the people's judgement always true;
The most may err as grossly as the few.

JOHN DRYDEN

I do not object to people looking at their watches when I am speaking. But I do strongly object when they start shaking them to make sure that they are still going.

LORD BIRKETT

Sir Leicester has no objection to an interminable Chancery suit. It is a slow, expensive, British, constitutional kind of thing.

CHARLES DICKENS
Bleak House

Justice is open to everybody in the same way as the Ritz Hotel.

JUDGE STURGESS

ROBERT LORD RAYMOND.

THE TRIAL OF DEEMING; MISS ROUNSVILLE GIVING EVIDENCE.

Judge: 'What do you suppose that I am on the Bench for, Mr Smith?'

F.E.: 'It is not for me to attempt to fathom the inscrutable workings of Providence.'

F.E. SMITH

The law of England is very strange: it cannot compel anyone to tell the truth ... But what the law can do is to give you seven years for not telling the truth.

MR JUSTICE DARLING

In sentencing a man for one crime, we may well be putting him beyond the reach of the law in respect of those crimes which he has not yet had an opportunity to commit. The law, however, will not be cheated in this way. I shall therefore discharge you.

N.F. SIMPSON

But he regards the Court of Chancery, even if it should involve an occasional delay of justice and a trifling amount of confusion, as a something, devised in conjunction with a variety of other somethings by the perfection of human wisdom, for the eternal settlement (humanly speaking) of everything.

CHARLES DICKENS
Bleak House

Much as he is opposed to law-breaking, he is not bigoted about it.

DAMON RUNYON

A judge is not supposed to know anything about the facts of life until they have been presented in evidence, and explained to him at least three times.

LORD CHIEF JUSTICE PARKER

It is much more difficult to judge oneself than to judge others.

ANTOINE de SAINT-EXUPÉRY

This case bristles with simplicity.

MR JUSTICE COMYN

Mr Justice Ridley was known as Mr Justice Necessity, since necessity knows no law.

FRANCIS PEARSON

It is a very salutary check for a judge to realise that if he does say something silly it is liable to get into the newspapers.

MR JUSTICE TEMPLEMAN

No one should be a judge in his own case.

PUBLILIUS SYRUS

Like to some magistrates grown gray in office
Calmly he contemplates alike the just
And unjust, with indifference he notes
Evil and good, and knows not wrath nor pity.

ALEXANDER PUSHKIN

As judges we are neither Jew nor Gentile, neither Catholic nor agnostic.

SIR ARTHUR STANLEY EDDINGTON

Middle Temple Hall

Sr. Wm. Dugdale.

from an Original in the Bodleian Gallery, Oxford.

How would you be,
If He, which is the top of judgement, should
But judge you as you are?
WILLIAM SHAKESPEARE
Measure for Measure

They were all exceedingly amused, and were more like people coming out of a Farce or a Juggler than from a Court of Justice.
CHARLES DICKENS
Bleak House

The judge is condemned when the criminal is absolved.
PUBLILIUS SYRUS

The cold neutrality of an impartial judge.
EDMUND BURKE

In some Central and South American countries if you are a judge, you are either very rich or you are in the cemetery.
Reported by DAVID WARD
President of the Law Society 1989–90

Policemen, like red squirrels, must be protected.
JOE ORTON
Loot

The South African Police would leave no stone unturned to see that nothing disturbed the even terror of their lives.
TOM SHARPE

Detectives are only policemen with smaller feet.
MARLENE DIETRICH

I guess I must have had New England ancestors away back and inherited some of their staunch and rugged fear of the police.

O. HENRY

Those who have conducted prosecutions on police evidence know the appalling risks which arise when the police approach a case with a preconceived notion of the guilt of the accused.

F.E. SMITH

I have never seen a situation so dismal that a policeman couldn't make it worse.

BRENDAN BEHAN

Excellent books are slippery things. They slip through the fingers of policemen who want to prevent them being published, and once they are in print, they slip out of the categories into which tidy-minded critics long to fix them.

CLARENCE BROWN

A doctor who doesn't say too many foolish things is a patient half-cured, just as a critic is a poet who has stopped writing verse and a policeman a burglar who has retired from practice.

MARCEL PROUST

For the urban poor the police are those who arrest you. In almost any slum there is a vast conspiracy against the forces of law and order.

MICHAEL HARRINGTON

CLIFFORD'S INN

Middle Temple Gateway from the Strand
Herbert Railton

I didn't like the police helmet. That's why I was hoping to get into the motor squad where I could have worn a flat cap.

GILBERT HARDING

I like to see policemen about the place, preferably large ones who have been at it long enough not to look embarrassed by their hats.

W.F. ELLIS

When constabulary duty's to be done,
The policeman's lot is not a happy one.

W.S. GILBERT
The Pirates of Penzance

One has to multiply thoughts to the point where there aren't enough policemen to control them.

S.J. LEE

A long line of cases shows that it is not merely important, but it is of fundamental importance, that justice should not only be done, but should manifestly and undoubtedly be seen to be done.

LORD HEWART

This is a British murder inquiry and some degree of justice must be seen to be more or less done.

TOM STOPPARD

Justice must not only be seen to be done. It must be seen to be believed.

J.B. MORTON

Justice, I think, is the tolerable accommodation of the conflicting interests of society, and I don't believe there is any royal road to attain such accommodations concretely.

PHILIP HAMBURGER

Extreme justice is extreme injustice.

CICERO

Hogan's r-right whin he says: 'Justice is blind'. Blind she is, an' deef an' dumb an' has a wooden leg.

MR DOOLEY

The price of justice is eternal publicity.

ARNOLD BENNETT

Justice is a machine that, when someone has once given it the starting push, rolls on of itself.

JOHN GALSWORTHY

Justice is being allowed to do whatever I like.
Injustice is whatever prevents me doing it.

SAMUEL BUTLER

Be not biased with compassion to the poor, or favour to the rich, in point of justice.

LORD CHIEF JUSTICE SIR MATTHEW HALE

Gateway to Middle Temple

"SHE STRUCK ONE OF HER WARDERS . . . A KNOCK-DOWN BLOW"

All the world's a stage,
And all the men and women merely players:
They have their exits and their entrances;
And one man in his time plays many parts ...
And then the justice,
In fair round belly with good capon lin'd,
With eyes severe, and beard of formal cut,
Full of wise saws and modern instances;
And so he plays his part.

WILLIAM SHAKESPEARE
As You Like It

Let justice be done though heaven should fall.

LUCIUS CALPURNIUS

SCREEN IN THE OLD HALL.

In the course of justice, none of us should see salvation.

WILLIAM SHAKESPEARE
The Merchant of Venice

The love of justice in most men is simply the fear of suffering injustice.

FRANÇOIS, DUC DE LA ROCHEFOUCAULD

Man's capacity for justice makes democracy possible, but man's inclination to injustice makes democracy necessary.

REINHOLD NEIBUHR

NEW HALL AND LIBRARY, FROM NEW SQUARE.

I am certain that nothing has done so much to destroy the juridical safeguards of individual freedom as the striving after this mirage of social justice.

FRIEDRICH AUGUST VON HAYEK

Pub. April 1 1800 by W. Richardson No 31 Strand.

The Temple Church.

Peace is more important than all justice; and peace was not made for the sake of justice, but justice for the sake of peace.

MARTIN LUTHER

I will be as harsh as truth and as uncompromising as justice. On this subject I do not wish to think, or speak, or write, with moderation. No! No! Tell a man whose house is on fire to give a moderate alarm: tell him to moderately rescue his wife from the hands of the ravisher; tell the mother to gradually extricate her babe from the fire into which it has fallen: but urge me not to use moderation.

WILLIAM LLOYD GARRISON

There is no such thing as justice – in or out of court.

CLARENCE SEWARD DARROW

It is justice, not charity, that is wanting in the world.

MARY WOLLSTONECRAFT

One man's justice is another's injustice; one man's beauty another's ugliness; one man's wisdom another's folly.

RALPH WALDO EMERSON

Poetic justice, with her lifted scale,
Where in nice balance, truth with gold she weighs,
And solid pudding against empty praise.

ALEXANDER POPE

Why has the government been instituted at all? Because the passions of men will not conform to the dictates of reason and justice, without constraint.

ALEXANDER HAMILTON

Recompense injury with justice, and recompense kindness with kindness.

CONFUCIUS

Justice without strength is helpless, strength without justice is tyrannical. Unable to make what is just strong, we have made what is strong just.

BLAISE PASCAL

The sword of justice has no scabbard.

JOSEPH DE MAISTRE

I shall temper so
Justice with mercy.

JOHN MILTON

Though justice be thy plea, consider this,
That in the course of justice, none of us
Should seek salvation: we do pray for mercy.

WILLIAM SHAKESPEARE
The Merchant of Venice

Thwackum was for doing justice, and leaving mercy to heaven.

HENRY FIELDING

Injustice anywhere is a threat to justice everywhere.

MARTIN LUTHER KING

Justice is truth in action.

BENJAMIN DISRAELI

PHILIP EARL of HARDWICKE.

Entrance Porch.

The Judge should not be young; he should have learned to know evil, not from his own soul, but from late and long observation of the nature of evil in others; knowledge should be his guide, not personal experience.

PLATO

How dreadful it is when the right Judge judges wrong.

SOPHOCLES

I am as sober as a Judge.

HENRY FIELDING

A witness cannot give evidence of his age unless he can remember being born.

JUDGE BLAGDEN

Is Christ thy advocate to plead thy cause?
Art thou his client? Such shall never slide.
He never lost a case.

EDWARD TAYLOR

Good counsellors lack no clients.

WILLIAM SHAKESPEARE
Measure for Measure

Surgeons are substantially helped, no doubt, by the extreme difficulty said to be experienced in obtaining a qualified medical opinion critical of another medical practitioner – a difficulty second only to that reputedly faced by an aggrieved litigant who tries to find a solicitor willing to undertake a case against another one.

BERNARD LEVIN

The good have no need of an advocate.
PHOCION

Many receive advice, few profit by it.
PUBLILIUS SYRUS

Nothing is given so profusely as advice.
FRANÇOIS, DUC DE LA ROCHEFOUCAULD

Advice is seldom welcome; and those who want it the most always like it the least.
EARL OF CHESTERFIELD

To marry is to halve your rights and double your duties.
ARTHUR SCHOPENHAUER

Divorce is the sign of knowledge in our time.
WILLIAM CARLOS WILLIAMS

Divorced couples hob-nobbed with each other, and with each other's co-respondents.
NOEL COWARD

Whoever looketh on a woman to lust after her hath committed adultery with her already in his heart.
MATTHEW 5:28

What men call gallantry, and gods adultery,
is much more common where the climate's sultry.
LORD BYRON

Crime is a left-handed form of human endeavour.
JOHN HUSTON

CHAMBERS IN OLD SQUARE.

The Trial

Arson, after all, is an artificial crime … A large number of houses deserve to be burnt.

H.G. WELLS

She'll commit every crime a respectable woman can.

GEORGE BERNARD SHAW
Man and Superman

I came to the conclusion many years ago that almost all crime is due to the repressed desire for aesthetic expression.

EVELYN WAUGH

He is capable of any crime, from reviling the classics to diverting water-courses.

ERNEST BRAMAH

When a doctor does go wrong he is the first of criminals. He has nerve and he has knowledge.

SIR ARTHUR CONAN DOYLE

Full many a vice is born to blush unseen. Full many a crime the world does not discuss.

SIR JOHN SQUIRE

Law and order is one of the steps taken to maintain injustice.

A. BONAR LAW

The only reason the crime rate was so low in rural areas such as this was the close-knit social structure. When everyone knows everyone else, crime was either difficult or desperate.

JOHN FOWLES

Society already understands that the criminal is not he who washes dirty linen in public, but he who dirties the linen.
VLADIMIR BUKOVSKY

Crime is common. Logic is rare. Therefore it is upon the logic rather than upon the crime that you should dwell.
SIR ARTHUR CONAN DOYLE

If he's a criminal, he's in plain clothes – that's all I can say.
N.F. SIMPSON

I wanted to be an arch-criminal as a child, before I discovered I was too short.
WOODY ALLEN

Authors and uncaptured criminals ... are the only people free from routine.
N. VACHEL LINDSAY

I read nothing except the criminal news and the agony column. The latter is always instructive.
SIR ARTHUR CONAN DOYLE

Men are not hanged for stealing horses, but that horses may not be stolen.
GEORGE SAVILE

But from each crime are born bullets that will one day seek out in you where the heart lies.
PABLO NERUDA

As witnesses not of our intentions but of our conduct, we can be true or false, and the hypocrite's crime is that he bears false witness against himself.
HANNAH ARENDT

NEW SQUARE, LINCOLN'S INN.

The Right Hon.[ble]

FRED.[K] EARL OF CARLISLE.

Lord Lieu.[t] of the Kingdom of Ireland

Crime like virtue has its degrees; and timid innocence was never known to bloom suddenly into extreme licence.

JEAN RACINE

No one becomes depraved in a moment.

JUVENAL

There is a method in man's wickedness – It grows up by degrees.

FRANCIS BEAUMONT AND JOHN FLETCHER

The only medicine for suffering, crime, and all the other woes of mankind is wisdom.

THOMAS HENRY HUXLEY

The atrocious crime of being a young man, which the honourable gentleman has with such spirit and decency charged upon me, I shall neither attempt to palliate nor deny, but content myself with wishing that I may be one of those whose follies may cease with their youth, and not of that number who are ignorant in spite of experience.

WILLIAM PITT, EARL OF CHATHAM

Popularity is a crime from the moment it is sought; it is only a virtue where men have it whether they will or not.

GEORGE SAVILE

Successful and fortunate crime is called virtue.

SENECA

In other countries poverty is a misfortune – with us it is a crime.

LORD LYTTON

It is worse than a crime, it is a blunder.
CHARLES DE TALLEYRAND

The greatest of evils and the worst of crimes is poverty.
GEORGE BERNARD SHAW
Major Barbara

Small habits well pursued betimes
May reach the dignity of crimes.
HANNAH MORE

He left a corsair's name to other times,
Linked with one virtue, and a thousand crimes.
LORD BYRON

History is indeed little more than the register of the crimes, follies, and misfortunes of mankind.
EDWARD GIBBON

O liberty! O liberty! What crimes are committed in thy name!
JEANNE MANON ROLAND
last words from the guillotine

The act is not criminal unless the intent is criminal.
LEGAL MAXIM

In a free society the state does not administer the affairs of men. It administers justice among men who conduct their own affairs.
WALTER LIPPMAN

THE CONDEMNED CELL IN NEWGATE.

AREA IN NEW SQUARE.

I chose justice ... I know that there is in it something that has meaning, that is man, for he is the only being who demands to have it.

ALBERT CAMUS

Stare decisis is usually the wise policy, because in most matters it is more important that the applicable rule of law be settled than it be settled right ... The Court bows to the lessons of experience and the force of better reasoning, recognising that the process of trial and error, so fruitful in the physical sciences, is appropriate also in the judicial function.

JUDGE BRANDEIS

There is danger that, if the Court does not temper its doctrinaire logic with a little practical wisdom, it will convert the constitutional Bill of Rights into a suicide pact.

ROBERT HOUGHWOUT JACKSON

There is a strange charm in the thoughts of a good legacy, or the hopes of an estate, which wondrously alleviates the sorrow that men would otherwise feel for the deaths of friends.

MIGUEL DE CERVANTES

I advise you to go on living solely to enrage those who are paying you annuities. It is the only pleasure that I have left.

VOLTAIRE

I have spent all my life under a Communist regime, and I will tell you that a society without any objective legal scale is a terrible one indeed. But a society with no other scale but the legal one is not quite worthy of man either.

ALEXANDER SOLZHENITSYN

After all, this is the Nation's ultimate judicial tribunal, not a super-legal-aid bureau.

FELIX FRANKFURTER

Time is a great legalizer, even in the field of morals.

H.L. MENCKEN

How amazing it is that, in the midst of controversies on every conceivable subject, one should expect unanimity of opinion upon difficult legal questions.

CHARLES EVANS HUGHES

Poets are the acknowledged legislators of the world.

PERCY BYSSHE SHELLEY

Title of a novel criticising British divorce laws – *Holy Deadlock*.

A.P. HERBERT

The history of scholarship is a record of disagreements. And when we deal with questions relating to principles of law and their applications, we do not suddenly rise into a stratosphere of icy certainty.

CHARLES EVANS HUGHES

Teach him what has been said in the past; then he will set a good example to the children of the magistrates, and judgement and all exactitude shall enter into him. Speak to him, for there is none born wise.

PTAHOTPE
c. 2350 BC

SERLE'S GATE, LINCOLN'S INN.

THE TRIAL OF CAPTAIN KIDD.

Do justice, that you may live long upon earth. Calm the weeper, do not oppress the widow, do not oust the man from his father's property, do not degrade magnates from their seats. Beware of punishing wrongly; do not kill, for it will not profit you.

KING OF HERACLEOPOLIS
to his son Merikare, *c.* 2000 BC

Confession is the queen of evidence.

ANDREI VYSHINSKY

When I came back to Dublin, I was court-martialled in my absence, and sentenced to death in my absence, so I said they could shoot me in my absence.

BRENDAN BEHAN

Tell the truth or trump – but get the trick.

PUDDENHEAD WILSON

Take nothing on its looks: take everything on evidence. There's no better rule.

CHARLES DICKENS
Great Expectations

Some circumstantial evidence is very strong, as when you find a trout in the milk.

HENRY DAVID THOREAU

There is no witness so dreadful, no accuser so terrible as the conscience that dwells in the heart of every man.

POLYBIUS

There's just ae thing I cannae bear, An' that's my conscience.

ROBERT LOUIS STEVENSON

There are three kinds of lies – lies, dammed lies and statistics.

MARK TWAIN

My guiding star always is, Get hold of portable property.

CHARLES DICKENS
Great Expectations

It is by the goodness of God that we have in our country three unspeakably precious things: freedom of speech, freedom of conscience, and the prudence never to practise either.

MARK TWAIN

Hogarth d.t *T. Clark sculp.t*

London Published as the Act directs by Robert Scholey 46 Paternoster Row.

Engraved by J. Jenkins.

EDWARD CLINTON, EARL OF LINCOLN.

OB. 1584.

FROM THE ORIGINAL OF KETEL, IN THE COLLECTION OF

HIS GRACE, THE DUKE OF BEDFORD.

Published by Harding Triphook & Lepard, Finsbury Square, London Dec. 1, 1824

Modesty can be cultivated until it becomes something very like a crime.

CHARLES TURLEY

Scholars dispute and the case is still before the courts.

HORACE

Most people judge men only by their success or their good fortune.

FRANÇOIS, DUC DE LA ROCHEFOUCAULD

You are young, my son, and as the years go by, time will change and even reverse many of your present opinions. Refrain therefore awhile from setting yourself up as a judge of the highest matters.

PLATO

Those who wish to appear wise among fools, among the wise seem foolish.

QUINTILIAN

A fool with judges, amongst fools, a judge.

WILLIAM COWPER

This man [Chesterfield], I thought, had been a lord among wits, but I find he is only a wit among lords.

SAMUEL JOHNSON

Commonly we say a judgement falls upon a man for something in him we cannot abide.

JOHN SELDON

Everyone complains of his memory, and no one complains of his judgement.

FRANÇOIS, DUC DE LA ROCHEFOUCAULD

Public opinion is stronger than the legislature, and nearly as strong as the Ten Commandments.

CHARLES DUDLEY WARNER

Let the punishment match the offence.

CICERO

No punishment has ever possessed enough power of deterrence to prevent the commission of crimes. On the contrary, whatever the punishment, once a specific crime has appeared for the first time, its reappearance is more likely than its initial emergence could have been.

HANNAH ARENDT

The broad effects which can be obtained by punishment in man and beast are the increase in fear, the sharpening of the sense of cunning, the mastery of the desires; so it is that punishment tames man, but does not make him 'better'.

FRIEDRICH WILHELM NIETZSCHE

Art is long, life short, judgement difficult, opportunity transient.

JOHANN WOLFGANG VON GOETHE

Life is short, the art long, opportunity fleeting, experience treacherous, judgement difficult.

HIPPOCRATES